Acknowledgements

Acknowledgements are now due to the editors of the following, in which some of the poems in this collection previously appeared: *The Irish Press*; *Open Drills*; *The First Cut*; *Burning Bush*; and, *Blueprint*.

Some were also broadcast on *Sunday Miscellany* on RTE Radio 1.

For John Wortley

Light bends through the January branches.
In the half-darkness, his imagination
whittles the fallen trunks of aged trees
into singing birds and curious ducks
whose every peck reveals the spring.

Contents

Three

Four

One

The Singing Dead

(Ballintubbert Churchyard)

i

All this long summer
the graveyard has gone on breathing,
the gentle dead inhaling gulps of golden air,
dog roses scenting the barley breeze,
while birds have choired without consideration of tomorrow.

ii

Listen for the murmuring voices
from every corner of this resting ground,
wakened by the warming wash of early sun.
Always the earth has opened here
taking the dead, like lovers, to its breast,
has never failed them,
never turned them once away.

iii

Listen to the voices of the singing dead,
as they make their own pure music.

iv

Hannah Boyle
goes, crooning quietly, about her work
and reads, again, the headstone words,
that label her as faithful and valued servant
of Thomas Kelly.
A young woman of twenty-two,
she glimpsed a life

that might have been.
One filled with hope, to overflowing.
But when she died, at eighty-eight,
she was still that faithful, valued servant of someone else's dreams,
still staunchly faithful to her own.

v

Tommy Doyle marches in his uniform
to the wall below the church,
inspects the two white horses
parading in the field –
a foal between them in the fragrant, purple clover –
and grins at life.
Whistling, he waits. The horses turn
and cross to nuzzle on his open, grassy hand.

vi

Midday and the shadows disappear,
each dipped beneath its lichened stone.
Paint curls, like a young girl's hair, on windowsills.
Them also which sleep in Jesus will God bring with him.
Isobel Lett, who lived for half a year,
Elizabeth Empey, lost at four,
sit daisy-chaining in the eager sun.
Forever with the Lord.
A scale of rust flakes from a thirsty gutter
and flitters to the gravelled ground.
Bees softly nest beneath the vestry slates
while, blade by blade, the shadows stretch their arms
and the voices sing again.

vii

Mary Sheil, who lived a hundred years in life,
has lived a hundred years in death.
She rings the bells of fuchsia near the wall
and hears her music,
in a crimson symphony of flowers tolling,
a melody that she still treasures most.

viii

Joe Meredith is smiling as he smiled
in the blazing spring of '84;
having lived a gentle life
he lives in gentle death.
Watching the harvest trailers pass the gate,
winding their way from South Field,
beneath a moon that makes a day of night,
he nods, approvingly, and hums a cheerful song.

ix

And the short summer night draws on.
High in the blue sky,
the tipsy weather-vane points east to heaven
and west to the earth
that opened to the pale, uncertain dead
and held them to its beating heart
when cuckoos sang
and corncrakes craaked in sorrel fields.

x

Joyce Hazel Pansy Graham skips away from her grandfather's hand,
rhyming her three-year childish song.
Stopping, she picks a pink and perfumed rose,
offering it to finches
and pigeons, whose swooping hymn she loves,
until they, too, fall silent in the evening breeze.
Trailing with tired slowness between the stones,
she hears her mother call her home,
to sleep where she forever sleeps.

xi

Listen to this silence.
It lies like ashes in a summer fireplace.

xii

Until.
Until, among the deepened shadows,
stepping between the noiseless tombs,
Abigail Meredith,
raises her girlhood voice
into the hazy twilight,
breathing the gentle breath of night
across this sinking summer day.

xiii

The day Lord thou gavest, now is ended
The darkness falls at thy behest
To thee our morning hymns ascended
Thy praise shall hallow now our rest.

Bogwoman

i

Something about her harks back to the bog
and a moonlit, summer night
with the sky opening itself
to whatever the darkness offers.

Something in the sad, momentary drift
of her eyes to the window,
hints at a day in February,
perhaps the last day of that month,

when the weather was wild as nakedness,
the wind tossing madly,
and no one could even guess
at the pain inside her heart.

She goes on searching for the laughter,
the promise of this long summer night.

ii

A summer Sunday at the start of singing June,
wet and warm, the sky a ball of lead.
I see her on the lane, her red umbrella
a shelter from the rain, the possibility of life.

Each afternoon she walks this path, to the very end,
to where the tar gives way and sinks into
the faltering hardcore and then into the
ninety-thousand years of turf and history with

its brides' bouquets of Columbine, its chronicles
of groping love, backbroken labour
and weighted flesh, buried like stones
in black bogholes by one passion or another .

And she never ventures out onto the bog. Instead, she looks,
and turns and walks back to her garden and her God.

iii

Onetime, a long time ago,
a man spoke to her in the twilight.
His voice was low and she had to strain
to catch his words above the breeze.

They were standing at the gable of a shed.
He said: *I want to kiss you, bogwoman,
I want to kiss your ears, your mouth, your neck,
your nipples, your belly, your thighs, your cunt.*

*Especially your cunt
where I can taste the way you fucked me.*
She knows that if she told someone,
they'd say she'd dreamt it all in some mad dream.

But this was not a dream,
this has a taste beyond imagination.

iv

Another time, a long way from home
and from the things that were familiar,
she saw an African woman at a bus stop
on the King's Road. It was summertime.

The woman's skin reminded her
of how the evening sky dilutes in bog pools,
letting its colours linger with the promise
of long days still to come. And she

walked up to the silent, motionless woman
and touched the side of her shining face
and the woman smiled and held her hand
for an enduring moment. Two souls at sea,

each far from a homeland and from a time
when life was more than simply memory.

v

The warm earth that is hardly earth
folds about the shadow of her skin.
The sun's hotness draws blood to her face
but her vision remains dead to its light.

A sudden breeze lifts and drops dark mould
in pools that were and will be stagnant;
the frozen heads of seeded cotton
nod and check and nod again.

The whole flat world is tanned,
Even the glint of sun off water
comes back mute. Her eyes are brown,
her skin, her hair, her fingernails.

She doesn't move, the kiss of heat
smiles on her smiling mouth.

An Octet for John Clare

i

Five days into summer
and the lilacs sing in the hedges,
cherries are snowing on every street.
So it will be all summer long.

ii

On the narrow path of a summer street,
they step away from quick and certain feet.
Uneasy now, their massive frames are less
impressive in a stumbling awkwardness.
But see these men in full red autumn fields,
among the harshness of slow, grudging yields,
sweating to lift the harvest they have cut,
essential to our lives as we are not.

iii

There is a hint of autumn in the hedges-
not in the woodbine, still smelling golden after rain,
nor in the blackberries which are hardly more than flowers
nor in Purple Loosestrife which climbs for the joy
of being in full flush. But something lurks
behind the leaves and in the water.
In the deep, dark dykes it whispers Autumn.

iv

The mighty spreading beech is gone,
great tree we almost swore upon.
Only the scabby stump remains.
We found it in the dusky rain.
We'd watched it reach its summer peak
and, later, still in half blown leaf.

This evening from the damp hilltop,
drawn down, we feel compelled to stop,
and count the redding rings of time.
One hundred and then sixty-nine.

v

Blackbird in the apple basket,
absorbed in morning's frenzied task,
the time of singing is long past.
Dark eye, knifed beak, bent feathered head,
intent on autumn's feast instead.
And spring's first buds, uncurled, lie dead.

vi

They call this light
the winter star,
its blaze is bright
and travels far,
it sits above
the empty fields
remembering
rich autumn yields.

vii

He loved the hare, the berried thrush,
he loved the sullen winter hush
of falling night at Christmas time.

He loved the sun at break of day,
and loved its last, brash, crimson ray
and hoped that she would always stay.

viii

The ringmaster stands, the charming fellow,
in his red top-hat and coat of yellow.
He calls every tune, he conducts the band,
while gripping his whip, clench-tight in his hand.
The animals jump, the animals dance,
disturbed by his smile, the nails in his glance.
Elephants stumble, cowed tigers don't roar,
for none is the creature he was before.

She Came Down the Murky Night

She came down the murky night,
a less than beautiful Ophelia,
under the eyes of sleeping cattle on Lord's Island.

At some point in that morning
she brushed away damp branches below
this house, grey willow lying fruitless in low water,
with a careless rolling of her arm,

a slow and lapping ecstasy.
The unconscious strokes of grace now gone,
her body recovering its distant awkwardness,
lorry drivers bullocked it ashore.

The Last Day of April

All night I've lain awake with this man on my mind.
I met him in the woods at sunset.
He, carrying fallen branches to his van,
and I, just going home.
Both of an age.

We stood together in the golden car park,
talking politics, ecology and, somehow or other, dancehalls.
His tired eyes were young again.
"I met a girl in that dancehall when I was twenty-three.
We were friends, good friend, for years,
twice we travelled to Courtown, to the sea."
Sucking deeply on his withered cigarette, he spoke her name.
"I still have her photograph.
I have a copy of a Christmas card she sent me.
She married someone else, had lots of kids."
He paused. His eyes were dying now.
"I'd love to see her...see her once again."

To drown the singing of the birds,
tolling out their lust for sex and land,
I stumbled something about life
but he had no call for conversation,
simply needing to be heard.

All night I've lain awake with this man on my mind,
that small word *else* bursting with might have been.

Driving to Meet Chris and Paddy Kinsella

I am driving back to the village where I was born,
an evening in mid-October
and the air is like summer.
A haze has camped on the side of Fraughan Hill
and the light keeps hanging on –
frozen in this glorious dusk,
refusing to fold into darkness.

And I'm back cycling this road,
all of thirty-five years have disappeared.
It's early summer,
the world is there before me,
sun shining day after day.
The summer a series of promises,
just waiting to be kept.

In the House We Used to Have

They were telling me about this great party,
back in the house we used to have
and I was thinking of the man next door, whose wife had died.
They kept saying: *Yeah, yeah but it was fucking great and we got ossified.*
I thought of him, lying up there in the back bedroom,
straining for some break in the darkness,
in a room that faces east.
Her ghost among the dahlias by the gate.

Sonnet for John Wortley in his Ninetieth Year

If, as they say, the world was different then,
what is it now but different yet again?
Much of the past is held inside your heart,
showing itself in ways you make an art
of everything. Your hedges neatly laid,
crops tended, logs all stacked and drills well made.
From your deft hands the animals run loose
finding a shape and life in woods you choose.
In lilac, birch, chestnut - alive, complete,
each creature breathes again its true heartbeat.

Feeling the warmth we know in being friends,
we're drawn mesmeric to you. In the end,
the knowledge gathered in your summer days
illumines us with its instinctive ways.

Goldsmith

He settles restlessly,
the twelve good rules fly like bats in the darkness,
whipped from the walls of every alehouse in his past.
He would trade memory for life.
Thigh deep in corn,
pausing on the elbow of a road, he caught the weight of hawthorn
and knew in that moment his ghost would never loiter in Westminister
but under a may bush on a wet spring evening,
understanding the language
little understood.
He smiles to know his words, his heart, his liver will be analysed.

In life the women upstairs are laughing viciously.
Dice rattle on the board
and his brain is racing,
the lines and phrases coming,
the poem like a haemorrhage
leaving no room, no energy for living.
He would trade fame for peace.

The city is not real,
his reality is the past,
not London or the steep streets of Edinburgh;
not the Bishop's examination; the legal offices; the smell of medicine.
He is back, flute in pocket,
on the wet street where children play.
Burke and Reynolds are less real than these skipping infants;
the obliging drunken women are the dream
and the dream of singing hedges is reality.
He would trade pleasure for release.

The edging ship for Leyden or Padua
awakens something momentarily
and out on the ocean

the regular waves
restore the ploughman to the furrow in the field.
Dining finely with Johnson and their lady friends
he turns so suddenly, stopped by laughter,
catching the last tapered echo
of an echo heard in Blackfriars –
faint but certain.
The October wind gathers
the midlands smells and voices
and drops them in his sleeping lap
but he wakes to the sound of footsteps on his grave.

He settles restlessly
and the earth closes about the broken machinery of his life,
the clay rattles in the space about his bones,
in the corner of his smile.
Free at last, his ghost, a peaceful Heathcliff,
strides the paths of this parish,
pausing in the shelter of this tree or this or this.

Midlands

It keeps whispering,
even when I'm not listening,
whispering something
to someone else,
telling sad secrets,
here on the shore between life and eternity.

And some of its stories
are lies and some are the honest truth
and some I'm not even sure
I really heard.
But it never stops its whispering,
here on the shore between eternity and life.

ii

Dead and gone,
all the harm you've done
sprinkled with cold water
buried under clay,
all the harm you've done,
blessed and put away
for now. For now.

iii

That strange sound
of straining ropes
biting the ground
at the edge of his grave.
In the red brown
sunlight I smiled,
he loved going down
and now he has, forever.

iv

It must be seven years
since he shot my dog.
But sometimes on foggy mornings
I still hear the gun reverberate
and afterwards the silence.
The same silence
I remember from way back then.

v

Downstairs
he was all smiles to everyone.
Can I get you another drink?
Are you sure you wouldn't like some more to eat?
Can I get you anything at all?
You know you only have to say?
But I couldn't live downstairs,
not all the time.

vi

I heard the phone ring
and then your voice
cajoling me,
inveigling me,
and I fell for it.

I remember the ring I gave you,
the ring I placed on your finger,
and the impression it left
on the side of my face.

There's a ring
around the moon tonight,
cajoling me
inveigling me,
I want to fall for it.

vii

I remember an afternoon,
early winter,
a low sun.
I was carrying timber
from the woodpile in the yard
and, in the lamplight within,
I glimpsed you poring over a book.
My heart skipped a beat
like it used to skip a beat
when we first met.
But then I remembered the rest of it.

viii

To see you
was to see the most handsome man on our street
and so well dressed
and such a smile.
You were the
warmth coming back off the summer footpath,
you were my happiness,
you were my love.
And over there
is the field where we made surreptitious love
and behind it
the deep black river.

Afternoon and Evening
Approaching Christmas

I acquiesced. The voice from the twilit radio said:
'The Christmas we get we deserve.'
Later, on a bitter but unseasonable line,
we watched the evening burst and shine.
Being cynical and eclectic, I chose
– without hope and God knows
why – a kind of perfect greeting
which, like love, loses in repeating.

Beyond the Second Gate

(For Ariana Ball)

I see you now beyond the second gate,
your infant features drawn in smiles
and staring out of photographs, years after us.
A coy child. Later, in reticent love.
Laughing in outright happiness with some young man.
And shy again.

The daffodils in the low field have bloomed
for the first time in a dozen years
– in mid March, too –
beneath the oaks and limes which struggle now,
bent more each year but willing, still, to coat themselves for you.

This evening, in a gap,
I found the earliest wild violets.
All nature presages a life of joy.

I see you now beyond the second gate with music playing.
Before you, like laneways,
peace, happiness and love lifelong.

Music

He dreams of a long, bright house
and it is always summer.
He hears her making music.
From her room a small sound drifts.

We Were Boys Then

We were boys then,
filled with the expectation of the age,
fired by the vastness of the desert,
by the voice in the burning bush,
by the cross on the peak of the crooked hill.

But now we are these other people,
not the ghosts our fathers were,
not old before our years.
We are something else,
men trapped between a time that was
and a future without certainty.

What do we wish for ourselves?
Long life and happiness,
the peace to be at ease with what we've done or not undone,
some morsel from the plate of youth,
the will to stay forever open to the possibilities of life and love,
of the time we call tomorrow.

And tonight?
Perhaps, tonight we wish, beyond all else,
for the gift of memory,
the strength to face the wilderness
and not allow our fearlessness become our fear.
A way to be the boys we were back then.

Dead Fox

Magpied innards
on a summer road,
a brighter red
than this lifeless coat.
Spilled sentences that speak
of a wild
short
life,
the music left
in an old concertina.

Two

Brother

(i.m. Jarlath MacKenna)

i

I am writing this poem in the pencil light
from a hospital door.
My brother lies sleeping,
his lungs opened and shut by machinery.
The shadow of my hand falls across this page
as the shadow of something less certain
falls over his damaged body.
I want to comfort him,
to be the reassuring one
as he so often was to me.
He who always found a way round things
but not round this.

In the car tonight,
on the five minute drive from his house to the hospital,
I heard that song, *Daniel*, in the summer darkness.

Dearest brother, only brother, I love you
for all the days we were together
and all the times we were apart.
Your kindness is a soft voice
smiling down the telephone line,
telling me everything will be alright.
I wish I could say the same for you
and know there was some truth in it.
Instead, the night draws on
and the moon retreats a degree or two
and we share this room as we once shared a room at home.
You talking in one bed,
me laughing in the other.
We are both silent now
but for the drive and draw of air into your wounded lungs
and the soft movement of my pen
across the pages of what's left of our lives together.

I close my eyes and hear the echo of your words,
the memory of my laughter,
that song coming in on the late night radio,
its notes across the empty car park,
its tenderness hanging in the slow Carolina night.

ii

The North Carolina buoys
keep calling your name through the summer night,
tolling its two syllables
out there in the misted light of the moon.
Out there, just beyond the place
where my eyes can be sure of what I see.
Listen!
There they are again.
Again, again,
across the water
and eastward
to home.

iii

I was driving down the warm summer coast of Carolina,
driving your car,
listening to the music you had left on the cd rack,
the songs you inadvertently chose for me to hear.
The last music you played was
all those hits from the sixties,
a time when you were young
and I was younger,
a time when we both had
so much to live for.

iv

Weeks later, deciding my life needs something,
I begin to sort the books that overflow,
falling from the shelves and easing out across the floor,
like a long sentence,
until there is no floor.
And there it is,
your postcard from Savannah,
book-marking someone's poems,
a dream among these other dreams:
"We can hit Savannah some weekend and Charleston.
Think you would enjoy.
The Brother."

Snap

The photograph I treasure most is the next one, taken on the lawn.
Behind us, the laburnum arches rain,
and beyond that a wall is caught in the white sunlight,
holding the fresh green timber of the window frames.
If you look hard, you can see, beyond the glass, a sturdy avocado
etched in the other light of the courtyard door.

This, of course, is after the winter sleet and you in your overcoat
standing in the damp kitchen, bellowing the fire
through the careful coal with an open newspaper.
Your eyes, I notice, are level with my own.
Then the ambulance like an arrest, a gruff nurse in the late ward,
and, wouldn't you know it, the car packs it in,
gears clotting, pocking the yard with thick slopped oil.

We're all smiling and you have your good suit on,
a red tie, and your hands clasped before you as always –
the same pose echoes in this album back to 1949.
We're all smiling like a football team
and, later, you're singing *Genevieve*.

This is the photograph I treasure most.

A Ghost in the Car

You need some respite, the doctor said.
It's not just advisable, it's imperative
and, I promise, you'll be home in weeks.
The clock ticked, the fire sang.

I found my father waiting –
Available but not enthusiastic.
A February afternoon,
not quite ripe with spring.
Familiar roads,
the ones he'd driven (twenty thousand times,
I reckoned) to work and home;
the ones I'd shared in schooldays,
allowed to steer the Morris Minor on the straight.
A great silence remained unbroken
even as we edged through the afternoon traffic.
Over the Barrow bridge and right, onto the Stradbally Road –
finally, turning through the hospital gates,
 grey famine roof against the blue.
Only then did he speak:
I never thought you'd put me in the County Home.
To my father, this was still the workhouse –
dumping ground for the unwanted, unrecognised, unkempt
and undesired.

He did come home that spring
But, in the berried autumn,
he was back again.
This time I didn't have the heart or soul –
what am I saying – I didn't have the courage
to drive him there.

I'd visit daily.
The Railway Ward, the nurses joked –
three old men, one hundred and thirty seven years of trains
    between them,
three rusting engines in a final siding.
And this time there was no going home.

Some days my father's ghost travels with me in my car,
some days we laugh,
but some days he reminds me
and I shiver at the thought.

Returning from Dances

Smell of slowly burning orange peel
reminiscent
of late nights, returning from dances.
The house quiet,
the fire dying,
last lingering of my mother's presence.
Why tonight
again?

Small Boy

The woman is writing.
Through the open door the tea things are ready.
The small boy enquires once, twice to catch her attention:
'What's your lucky number?'
Without thinking, she gives him her birth date.
Later, he's away for messages,
milk bottles clattering in the rope bag.
In the dusk, he gives his horse a favourite name
and the number she offered him,
racing from pole to pole against the evening cars.
He knows nothing about absence,
about the envelope for the morning post.

Among the Trees

You, hanging feeders
among the trees. The birds in
flocks about your head.

Any news?

(for Ewan)

My son phones from the city
and says, as he always does:
"Well, any news?"
"No news," I say or
if there is some
I give him every detail of the local happenings.

One day he will phone
and someone else will answer
with the news.

The winter cherry, almost certainly, will be in bloom
and the daffodils or dandelions,
bluebells ringing or foxgloves.
The orchard wearing a floral wreath
or decked in Christmas frost
but none of this will be, that day,
the major source of news.

The Railway Yard

The railway yard at nine o'clock,
the darkest night of winter time.
Late trains are running later
and frost is polishing the rails.
No signal box, no crane on the siding,
instead the rows of empty cans.
Everything has changed
since that Christmas long ago
when my father walked this platform
and my brother came on the last train
from Dublin. They're both dead now
and I sit here waiting patiently for you,
dreaming of Advents that are past
and the long summers still to come.

The Day You Left

(for Eoin O'Flaithearta)

The day you left
the sun shone and the wind blew
fits and gales,
trees slapping the blue sky,
an autumn day remembering summer.
In the sun-trap of the courtyard at my workplace
wasps blew backwards across the grass,
in a final desperation.

You were in that city by the sea,
a new place filled with possibilities.
I imagined waves cresting the harbour wall.
My heart envied you
and wished you only well.

I was a man who had left orchards
and sadness
in my wake
but some day, in another, newer year,
the trees will break into blossom
rising on a warmer, lighter breeze
and you will recognise the fruit in them.

Dunnock

Needing to understand
why one dunnock dies
and another flies free from the jaws of death
is at the heart of who we are.

Mostly, the things we take to be important
are less so after all.
The thing that breeds unease
is the thing of true importance.

The thing that unsettles us,
that urge to know
the lie of land across deep water
is what truly matters.

Nothing becomes the human heart like doubt.
The painter's uncertain stroke,
the dancer missing her step,
the recognition of passion in a poet's line

remind us of where we are going and, more importantly, of how.
In our uncertainty, we may locate
the hidden roots
from which we come.

Each dunnock is caught in a different light
but light is the thing,
the dark light of flying, the brighter light of dying,
while we go on searching for who we are.

Three

Haiku Calendar

i

Beyond the half door
could be anything. For now
my hands cup your breasts.

ii

The tractor roars and
slows, turning in a spray of
swirling paper gulls.

iii

Soft, ineffective
light. A sky of melted slate
hardens after dark.

iv

In this room it is
silent. Outside, an orange
sliced in smoke, the moon.

v

Lambent, the cherries
drench their heavy breasted sweat
in lingam grasses.

vi

So much yellow now –
heartsease, primrose, oxeye and,
in the winter, this.

vii

The phone continues
silent, whispering: 'the past
is an old story.'

viii

Helianthin. More
foggy wedding snaps, porches
clipped. Dry, nusty leaves.

ix

Crick. Above my head
laburnum pods split in the
unexpected heat.

x

Jug of yellow flags,
sheet soaked in sweat and seed. Rich,
languid memories.

xi

Wind on the corner,
teenage coats flap about each
other. Love, oh love.

xii

Frost. Inside the hall,
where logs spit scented light, she
knows the story's end.

Billboard Haiku

Ger loves Sally so
fuck off and leave them alone.
Dante. Beatrice.

Haiku Sequence

(for Lydia)

i

The doors hang open.
An empty barn is filled with
sun, motes dance and dance.

ii

Love, not sacrifice,
I want, he said. Knowledge and
not a holocaust.

iii

The still hammock fills
with leaves, a weight of winter
on their shrivelled backs.

iv

Moon. Mountain. Lake. We
would remember this at death.
Do you remember?

v

I watch. Nothing moves
but the horizon becomes
something imagined.

vi

A child's first winter
smile. Morris dancers merging
on a damp King's Road.

Four

Willow Pattern

Working in the garden
he uncovers a shard of someone else's life.
He wants her to have it,
not because of its uncertain history
but as a kind of pledge
against the doubts
that constantly besiege them.

Next Morning

This house is like a morgue
since you left.
The bedroom door is still ajar,
waiting for you to close it.
And the armchairs face each other,
without a word to say.

Sometimes

Sometimes the night is
too long and sometimes the night
is not long enough.

Church

We'd seen the church a dozen times
by day and floodlit in the evenings,
its lines of crooked sentinels, dependable as centuries;
angled shadows from the well-placed lights.
And so we stepped inside the open gate,
crossing the hoary, frozen grass,
and found, instead of stony elegance,
a stolid building, like a threat,
an ugly sign nailed to the door:
Vehicles parked at owners' risk.

I was relieved by this reminder,
not everything is as it first appears
and we may yet, in spite of all I've done,
achieve the life we set inside our dreams

River

They sat in her car
on the bank of an autumn river
and she talked to him of truth.
Outside, the trees
were peeling off the summertime,
getting back to basics.

Her words flooded
through his head,
no room in there for words of his own.
She told him she
was one of the few
true believers.

And now another truth lies between them,
hard to handle,
as a body too long in water.
He thinks of Pilate
and that sad question,
Quid est veritas?

Spin the Bottle

I don't *do* pubs.
Too many ghosts hanging about,
their mouths grown slack or crooked,
their laughter raucous,
too much of an edge that's on the rim of violence
or self-pitying sentimentality.
Too many exaggerations
and wasted stories of lost opportunities,
always someone else to blame.

I don't *do* pubs
because I know the situation well enough by now.
It could as easily be me there on the high stool
and that's not where I want to be.
Of course, I don't have the morning-after excuses.
I can't produce the nights before
as some kind of spirited absolution or mitigation,
the laughing badge of laudable forgetfulness.
There is no fog through which to tell
grim tales of being *hammered, wasted, rat-arsed, pissed.*

I don't *do* pubs,
too many senseless poltergeists
amused by lost weekends,
forgotten fucks,
misplaced lives.
I have my own ghosts here.
The ones who reek of alcohol I leave elsewhere
because I have no time for them
and live in fear of where the bottle spins.

After My Brother Died...

I gave my soul to loneliness;
I gave my body to fear;
I went to dark places from which I've never quite come back;
I longed for a warm, slow stroll with him, across the evening beach;
I longed for one last long late-night conversation;
I tried to dream but the dreams refused to run;
I wore his shirt;
I went to where his ashes lie and I listened but no one spoke;
I was desolate;
I doubted everything but most of all I doubted me;
I woke up suspecting the truth;
I went on living day to day;
I worked;
I laughed and then resented my laughter;
I tried to pray but my prayers were a paper in the wind;
I drove past the old house and stared at the empty window of
    the room that had been ours;
I tried to understand;
I decorated the Christmas tree;
I threatened my son on Christmas day and afterwards I hugged him;
I lost my mind but the loss was not so great;
I wanted to believe;
I wanted my brother's faith, his hope, his great belief in the
    things that we'd been taught;
I wanted him to be, just that, simply to have him here;
I walked each day through hedges of Quince;
I was fearful and then I was afraid of my fear;
I was afraid;
I wanted never to forget;
I longed for forgetfulness;
I kept his email address on my computer;
I kept his phone number in my book;
I framed his photograph and photographs of the two of us together;
I played the music that he loved;

I walked and walked, as though he might be waiting in the forest;
I watched my dog for signs of some sixth sense;
I lost the place that divides need and want;
I cried;
I was afraid of how we grow to be the very thing we fear.

Where Sadness Begins

There is a place
where sadness begins –
a quiet corner
at the back of some unfashionable grocery shop;
a small, slumbering town
where people are busy – fixing cars, running, making love.

As often as not, the sun is shining,
though now and then it rains,
and the climate, like the people,
appears predictable.
We know this
because we live here

and are familiar with its general banality.
But, once in a blue moon, we can identify the room,
the leafy gateway or the freshly painted house
where our sadness began.
Occasionally, we know the reasons for such beginnings
or the absence of a reason.

Mostly, we muddle through,
putting the whole thing down to tiredness,
overwork, a lack of sleep.
Until someone else's sadness overcomes them
and we have a momentary recognition
of the empty place inside each heart.

JOHN MACKENNA is the author of seventeen books – short-stories, novels, memoir, history and biography. He is a winner of the Irish Times Fiction Award; the C Day Lewis Award; the Hennessy New Irish Writing Award and his most recent novel, *The Space Between Us*, was short-listed for the Kerry Book of the Year Award. His books have been translated into several languages. He is also a winner of a Jacob's Radio Award for his documentary work with the poet and songwriter Leonard Cohen. He teaches in NUI Maynooth.